Egyptian Treasures

Catherine Chambers

Published 2009 by
A & C Black Publishers Ltd.
36 Soho Square, London, W1D 3QY
www.acblack.com

ISBN HB 978-1-4081-0852-9
PB 978-1-4081-1298-4

Series consultant: Gill Matthews

This book is produced using paper that is made from wood grown in managed, sustainable forests. It is natural, renewable and recyclable. The logging and manufacturing processes conform to the environmental regulations of the country of origin.

Produced for A & C Black by Calcium.
Printed and bound in China by C&C Offset Printing Co.

All the internet addresses given in this book were correct at the time of going to press. The author and publishers regret any inconvenience caused if addresses have changed or sites have ceased to exist, but can accept no responsibility for any such changes.

Acknowledgements
The publishers would like to thank the following for their kind permission to reproduce their photographs:
Cover: Shutterstock. **Pages:** Alamy Images: The London Art Archive 11b; Corbis: Burstein Collection 9b, Werner Forman 17, 18, Free Agents Limited 19, David Lees 10, Gianni Dagli Orti/The Picture Desk Limited 9t, Roger Wood 14; Dreamstime: David Campbell 4, Katy Odell 8br, Asier Villafranca 21; Fotolia: Freesurf 15t, Travis Hiner 20, Horticulture 13, Stanislav 12; Shutterstock; Adam36 8bl, Robert J. Beyers II 8t, Mario Bruno 6, 16, Stephen Coburn 5b, Dainis Derics 7, Fatih Kocyildir 11t, Ulrich Willmünder 5t.

CONTENTS

WHAT IS TREASURE?

Ancient Egypt's treasures help us look deep into the past. Each treasure is part of a puzzle that builds a picture of people's lives. Most treasures are **artefacts**, which are objects that people have made from many different materials. There would be no artefacts without one huge feature – the River Nile.

The treasure of the Nile

Ancient Egypt grew up around its greatest treasure – the River Nile. People settled along its wide banks over 7,000 years ago. They came with their herds of animals because the grasslands of North Africa had turned to desert.

Traders **used the Nile to carry their goods to far-off lands.**

Fertile land

Every year, the Nile **floodwaters** brought down rich, fertile soil. This soil was great for growing crops. Some people sold crops they didn't need. This meant they grew wealthy and became powerful rulers.

Some artefacts are made of gold and precious jewels - others simply of wood or stone.

Precious pyramids

Egypt's kings and queens employed people to make useful and beautiful things. These are the artefacts that tell us so much about ancient Egypt. Many of them can be found in the kings' and queens' tombs, such as the great pyramids.

TRACKING TIME

Crops had to be planted at the right time of year, after the great River Nile had flooded. Farmers used a simple measuring rod to tell them when this was going to happen.

Measuring the seasons

The measuring rod was made from a tall **reed**. Notches were cut along its length. The farmer pushed the reed down into the river bed. The waters rose or fell against the notches. From this, the farmer could divide the year into three four-month seasons.

Farmers sowed crops, such as papyrus, when the river waters died down.

What is it to us?

The measuring rod was like a calendar – it divided the year into seasons. The modern-day calendar came from this early idea.

Star constellations
and zodiac signs

36 ten-day periods are
represented by people

Burying time

Later, ancient Egyptians wanted to
measure time more accurately. So they
invented a calendar, like the one above.
They studied the stars, moon, and sun
cycles to get it right. We divide our year
into 12 months. The Egyptians divided
theirs into 36 ten-day periods.

Tomb calendars told a dead
person's soul what season it was,
and if it was day or night. Some
of the best calendars have been
found painted on tomb walls.

HARVEST HELPERS

The sickle was a tool used by the ancient Egyptians to clear land to grow crops and flowers. Millions of simple sickles helped to produce enough food to sell to other lands. That made Egypt rich. The sickel was also used to cut reeds.

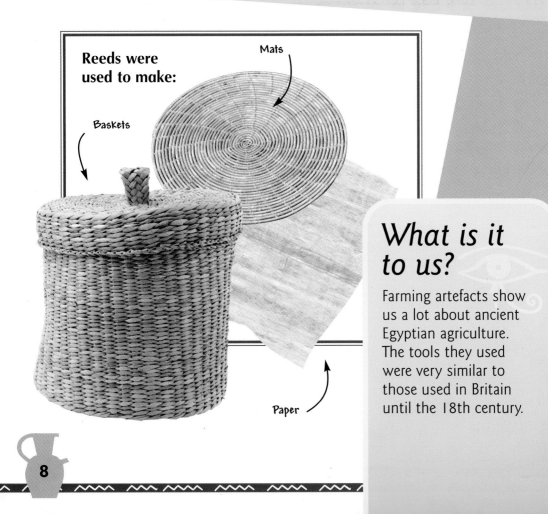

Reeds were used to make:

Mats

Baskets

Paper

What is it to us?

Farming artefacts show us a lot about ancient Egyptian agriculture. The tools they used were very similar to those used in Britain until the 18th century.

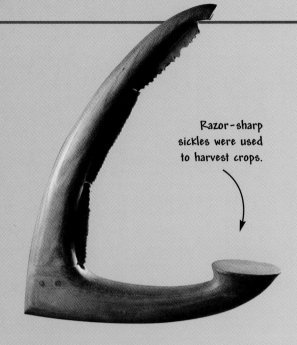

Razor-sharp sickles were used to harvest crops.

Tools for toil

Most sickles had a long, curved blade made of wood. A groove ran along the length of the blade. This groove was studded with small, razor-sharp **flints**. Many ancient sickles have been found. They were also painted on pots and walls in tombs.

More than one job

Grinding stones crushed wheat into flour. These useful tools were even placed inside pyramids, so the pharaohs' slaves could use them in the afterlife.

Labourers worked the land during the farming season. When the fields were flooded, they built great houses, temples, and pyramids. Their tools were also used for more than one task. A hoe dug up soil, but it could also be used to mix up clay to make bricks.

TOOLS OF THE TRADE

The pyramid at Giza is about 145 m (475 ft) tall. It's amazing how ancient Egyptians designed such huge pyramids and temples. Their architects and high priests had to draw very accurate diagrams. The most precious tool was the measuring rod.

Rods and lines

Like ancient Egyptian farmers, architects too had a measuring rod. However, this rod was used to measure height and width when designing buildings. The rod was a "royal cubit" long. That's from your elbow to the tip of your middle finger. Seven lines were carved along its length. Each was a hand-palm's width apart. Tiny measurements were marked in between, to make measuring more accurate.

Most rods were made of wood, with a hinge. The great architect, Kha, was buried with a rod of gold.

Mighty measures

- A *neibu* measured 1.5 times a royal cubit.
- A *het* measured 100 royal cubits.
- An *iteru* measured 20,000 royal cubits. That's about 10.5 km (6.5 miles).

From rods to arithmetic

Pyramids and temples were huge. The rod was too small to measure out such big heights and lengths. So architects had to work them out. They developed **arithmetic** and **mathematics** using a decimal system, just like we do today.

The pyramids are one of the world's mathematical marvels.

Scribes **and traders also begin using mathematics in their** accounts.

What is it to us?

Our mathematics developed from ancient Egyptian arithmetic. We could do very little today without it!

WEAPON WARFARE

Ancient Egypt's rulers kept sending soldiers to gain more territory. They also brought back precious items, such as wood, cosmetics, gold, and other treasures from far-off lands. All this wealth made other kingdoms jealous. So Egypt had to defend its borders well. Their main weapon for hundreds of years was the spear.

Weak weapons – enormous armies

Thousands of soldiers with spears sound really scary. The truth is that the spear was weak and slow. That's why armies had to be so enormous. Early spears were wooden poles with sharpened copper heads. By about 2000 BC, bronze heads made spears stronger. There were bronze-headed battle axes, too.

Bowmen could shoot while travelling very fast.

Beaten by technology

In 1700 BC, ancient Egypt learned the hard way that it needed stronger weapons. The Hyksos tribe came thundering into Egypt on chariots. They carried flexible bows that shot arrows far and fast. The Egyptians were forced to develop great chariots and better weapons of their own.

Soldiers were so important to the ancient Egyptians that hundreds of soldier statues were buried with pharaohs to protect them in the afterlife.

WRITTEN WONDERS

Writing was the best tool for organizing trade, government, religion, and just about everything in ancient Egypt. Hundreds of writers, or scribes, were employed throughout the empire. They wrote mountains of records, lists, and accounts. A scribe's most precious tool was his writing **palette**.

Writing tools

The writing palette was a bit like a small desk. It was wooden with two deep holes used as inkwells. These held powdered colours called pigments. Pens lay flat along a carved slender groove.

Being able to read and write were skills to be proud of in ancient Egypt. Some pharaohs had sculptures made that showed them reading or writing.

A scribe's toolkit

Papyrus paper was expensive to make, so it was used only for very important documents. Scribes first used **hieroglyph** pictures to represent words, then words and sounds. Later, they wrote in **hieratic** script, with a symbol for each letter.

Scribes wrote on:

- polished pottery
- stone
- clay tablets
- papyrus

Lozenge shapes were drawn around names of gods, kings, and queens

What is it to us?

We can learn about ancient Egypt's daily life, trade, religion, and politics from its written documents.

Egyptians first wrote about gods, kings, and queens.

15

MAKING MUSIC

Kings and wealthy merchants had a lot of spare time and money to hold magnificent parties and festivals where they listened to music. The oldest and best-loved musical instrument was the harp.

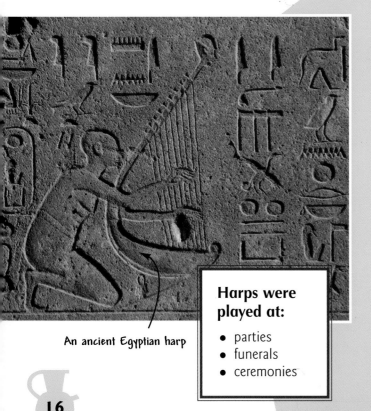

An ancient Egyptian harp

Harps were played at:

- parties
- funerals
- ceremonies

Music in life – and in death

There were many types of harp. Small ones were played so that musicians could dance at the same time. There were also huge harps, which were shown painted on tomb walls. They were the kind played at kings' funerals.

Some harps had only four strings, while others had as many as 22. Egyptians thought that harps were important to the gods. This is why so many kings' tombs had pictures of **harpists**.

Public performance

Kings also showed their power by holding musical processions. In these, soldiers performed powerful fighting dances as the bands played. Bands also performed at great public funeral processions for kings.

What is it to us?

Music became a symbol of wealth and power in our own royal courts. Even today, military bands play during parades.

The woman on the far right of this picture is playing a reed instrument called a *shawm*. The other women are clapping.

BEAUTIFUL BODIES

Almost every man and woman had at least one small blue pottery jar. These jars contained perfumed oils. There were also pots, palettes, grinders, and sticks for all kinds of cosmetics.

Looking good, feeling fine

Ancient Egyptians believed that the body, mind, and spirit were all connected. So it was important to look after the body. Both rich and poor used perfumed oils and **henna** for the hair. There were even expensive anti-wrinkle creams, treatments for baldness, and books on diets.

The ancient Egyptians stored their cosmetics in blue pots, such as this one.

Eye-catching

Eyes were very important. The ancient Egyptians used images of eyes for protection against evil. Dark **kohl** eyeliner made the eyes look larger. They also thought it protected the eyes from infection and insects. Kohl was made from galena, a mineral found around Mount Sinai. Green eyeshadow came from copper **ore**.

Eye make-up was put on perfectly. Ancient Egyptians used polished silver, copper, or bronze mirrors to make up their faces.

What is it to us?

Ancient Egyptians thought beauty was inside us as well as on the surface. Many of us believe that today. We also still use henna to colour and condition hair and kohl as eyeliner.

MYSTERIOUS MUMMIES

Mummies found inside ancient Egypt's tombs show us how bodies were prepared after death. Their **body tissues** tell us about the kinds of diseases they had. Their stomach contents and teeth show us the foods they ate. What amazing, gruesome treasures these are!

Looking good, feeling... rather dead!

Ancient Egyptians believed strongly in life after death. So they preserved the bodies of the dead in cloths.

Masks painted to show the face of the dead person were often placed on mummies.

Tools to prepare bodies:

- knives
- scalpels
- scissors
- pliers
- saws

Because the insides of bodies rotted, tools were later made to cut out the heart, liver, kidneys, and other organs. A long instrument like a knitting needle pulled the brain out through the nostril! All these organs were placed in tall **Canopic jars**.

The mummies of kings and queens were placed in painted tombs, such as this one.

What is it to us?

Many ancient Egyptian surgical instruments are used today to help cure living bodies.

GLOSSARY

accounts sums that add up what has been bought, sold, or made

arithmetic adding, subtracting, division, and multiplication

artefacts objects that people used a long time ago

body tissues a body's skin, flesh, and organs

Canopic jars a tall jar that held body parts. It had a stopper shaped like a human head

flints very smooth stone

floodwaters waters that swell with lots of rain or melted snow

grinding stones stones used to grind cereals or spices into a fine powder

harpist a person who plays a harp

henna a leafy plant that makes hair shiny and gives it a red colour. It can also be used to paint beautiful patterns called *mendhi* on the hands and feet

hieratic an ancient Egyptian form of writing that used characters rather than pictures

hieroglyph picture that has a meaning. Hieroglyphs were used in the same way that we use letters in words

kohl a black powder used to line the eyes

mathematics use of adding, subtracting, division, and multiplication to work things out

ore metals like gold or iron that are found in rock

palette a thin, flat board on which to lay out instruments or dab paints

papyrus a waterside plant and the paper made from the flattened, dried pith inside the plant

reed long, tall thick grass that grows at the water's edge

scribes writers who are paid to write letters, accounts, and other documents

traders people who buy, sell, or exchange goods

FURTHER INFORMATION

Websites

Read more about Ancient Egypt on these fun websites:

www.egypt.mrdonn.org

www.ancientegypt.co.uk/menu.html

www.historyforkids.org/learn/egypt

Books

100 Facts on Ancient Egypt by Jane Walker.
  Miles Kelly Publishing (2008).

100 Things You Should Know About Ancient Egypt
  by Jane Walker. Miles Kelly Publishing (2007).

Arts and Crafts of Ancient Egypt by Ting Morris.
  Franklin Watts (2006).

Gods and Goddesses of Ancient Egypt. by L. Ashworth.
  Evans Publishing Group (2001).

INDEX